THE

BEAUTIFUL

DESIGN

Marriage, Divorce, and the Gospel

Micheal and Rachel Pardue

The Beautiful Design
© 2018 by Micheal and Rachel Pardue
www.michealpardue.com
Published by:

Icard, NC
www.educationaldd.com

ISBN: 978-0-9986376-2-4

To Rachel

May our marriage always reflect God's desire for our hearts and life

CONTENTS

Acknowledgments   i

Preface   ii

1   What Shall We Think of Marriage?   1

2   Flippant Attitudes   6

3   Hard Hearts   14

4   God's Design for Marriage   20

5   The Consequences of Divorce   29

6   Moving Forward   36

7   The Gospel in Marriage   48

ACKNOWLEDGMENTS

We want to thank our parents who have model marriage for us. They have weathered tough times and demonstrated love when we fear many others would have fled. We also want to thank First Baptist Icard for making marriage a priority. That commitment has made this book all the more important for our church.

PREFACE

THE STATE OF MARRIAGE

It was just three years ago that we published the first edition of this book under the title *What God Has Joined Together*. I (Micheal) had preached much of this book during a sermon series through Mark's Gospel and the sermon, through divine providence, fell just a few weeks after the infamous *Obergefell v. Hodges* ruling was handed down by the Supreme Court of the United States. This decision legalized so called same-sex marriage across the whole of the United States. Many pastors immediately changed what they would be preaching that next Sunday, rightly criticizing this ruling that is both morally and legally flawed. I, however, stuck to my same preaching schedule, knowing that as I attempted to rightly divide the Word of God, He was bringing us to Mark 10 and it would be His Word that would shape our view of marriage.

This second edition, is not, however, a response to that ruling. There are great resources available if you are wanting to explore more on the marriage debate that is currently ravaging our churches and culture. This book is on an issue that seems to be largely settled in our culture—divorce. The battle looks to be lost. We write as the voice of lament, looking over the aftermath. We believe the cultural decline lamented in the current literature on marriage is a result of our own neglect of marriage in the Church of the Living God. We are deeply concerned about the rise of alternative views of sexuality. Homosexuality and transgender causes are confronting us on a daily basis. Christians must reject these as false idols of a fallen world. However, we must offer a clear alternative to the sexual idolatry of our age. We do this through Gospel-focused, Gospel-saturated marriages among those who claim the name of Christ. That is our greatest weapon against the latest attempt by the Enemy to destroy the families that the Lord so loves.

Since our first edition, we have seen the ugliness of divorce in ways that we had not previously experienced. We have had friends and family find their marriages torn apart. Children who were accustomed to mommy and daddy tucking them in at night, now bounced between two homes, sometimes uncertain about where they will lay their heads at night. Friends, our marriages are too important not to receive our care. They are too important to be sacrificed on the altar of the sexual revolution. Let us be concerned with how our society treats marriage and how it distorts sex. But let us first be concerned with how we honor Christ in the marriages that He has created!

Micheal and Rachel Pardue
December 2018

1

WHAT SHALL WE THINK OF MARRIAGE?

Not long ago I (Micheal) received a call from a friend seeking pastoral advice. This man has experienced deep loss as his family has been torn apart by divorce. His wife left him, taking their two young children. He has battled despair, uncertain of his future. He called me, his relationship with Christ suffering from this terrible tragedy, looking for help. He felt far from God and in many ways disenfranchised from the church.

He wanted my thoughts and advice as he struggled forward in what was already a difficult life, now complicated further by a broken home and broken marriage. The options I could provide him were very limited because this deep pain he is feeling is something that, quite frankly, will never go away. This man, who I personally baptized and ordained as a deacon, was struggling to make sense of his life and that will likely not change.

Divorce in our culture has become commonplace. Pick up a tabloid paper at the grocery store and you can read along as relationships are destroyed. Turn on the television and see lives ripped apart, seemingly for the entertainment of the masses. Musicians, actors, athletes, politicians; pick a category of celebrity and you will quickly find the ugliness of divorce. The normality of divorce has quickly given rise to a further distortion of marriage. So called same-sex marriage is now legal in our country. Lawsuits have already been filed demanding that polygamy and polyamory be legal expressions of sinful sexual desire. Christians are naïve if they believe there is an end to the distortion that the human mind can conjure up when it comes to sexual rebellion against God and His design for human relationships.

While we believe it is dishonest to act as if

this wave of relational destruction is new, it is by far the largest wave to roll ashore in our lifetime. The tide seems to creep more ominously up the beach each time a new fad or shift in sexual identity comes aground. The tsunami is reaching our culture in a way that previous generations did not envision and far too many in the church have fallen victim to the onslaught. The geography of morality has seen a momentous redesign and there appears no chance that our culture will return to previously drawn boarders.

What then are the people of God to think about divorce and this sexual revolution? What does God say to His people about divorce? What about those of you who are divorced? What is your usefulness in the Kingdom? How do Christians guard against divorce? These are important questions that the people of God must answer. The Bible is not silent on these issues. God has spoken frankly and at length to all of these and so many more questions about sexuality and relationships. He is does not remain silent and neither should His people. Silence will be of no assistance to the culture that is struggling to make sense of what is happening.

There are myriads and myriads of issues facing the contemporary Church. There are very few of them that are unimportant. This one, however, has come upon us quickly. It has gained speed and crashed upon us, demanding believers respond. In this, the followers of Christ must be found faithful, for our own sake and for the sake of the Kingdom of Christ.

In this brief work, we will examine Mark 10 as Jesus confronts a question about divorce from the religious leaders who are trying to trick Him into teaching something against God's Word. This text is just one of many that is concerned with marriage, the family, and the tragedy of divorce. Jesus' words are firm. Many have tried to lessen their blow. We have tried to avoid doing that. We deal with His words as true and relevant. This passage is timely. The epidemic of broken homes and relationships should demand that we, as followers of Christ, rise up to protect our own marriages, setting them forth as images of God's design when He created marriage and said, "It is good."

Mark 10:1–12 ESV:

And he left there and went to the

region of Judea and beyond the Jordan, and crowds gathered to him again. And again, as was his custom, he taught them.

And Pharisees came up and in order to test him asked, "Is it lawful for a man to divorce his wife?" He answered them, "What did Moses command you?" They said, "Moses allowed a man to write a certificate of divorce and to send her away." And Jesus said to them, "Because of your hardness of heart he wrote you this commandment. But from the beginning of creation, 'God made them male and female.' 'Therefore a man shall leave his father and mother and hold fast to his wife, and the two shall become one flesh.' So they are no longer two but one flesh. What therefore God has joined together, let not man separate."

And in the house the disciples asked him again about this matter. And he said to them, "Whoever divorces his wife and marries another commits adultery against her, and if she divorces her husband and marries another, she commits adultery."

2

FLIPPANT ATTITUDES

I (Micheal) love the word flippant. It just rolls off your tongue. Wrapped up in the word is a lot of meaning and being called flippant is a harsh insult indeed. A flippant attitude is often communicated within our common vernacular with the term, "whatever." Find a young person today and you can hear this term used for multiple responses that express a flippant attitude. If you scroll through the text-message exchanges of we exchange, it might read something like this:

Rachel: What do you want for supper?
Micheal: Whatever

Micheal: Where do you want to eat?
Rachel: Whatever

Micheal: What do you want to do today?
Rachel: Whatever

See a pattern? The response seems to indicate that the answer is unimportant. Interestingly, we both will use the term even when we do care about the answer but want the other person to make the decision.

Our culture has adopted a more dismissive definition than we typically exchange. The term is used to dismiss another person's words. Now, when someone says something you do not like or do not agree with, the response is simple: "Whatever!" No debate or argument. No courteous discussion. If you do not like it…"whatever!" It serves well as a response because it is so versatile for those who are flippant to anything and anyone.

A 2016 study found that "whatever" was the most irritating word for in the English language (eight years in a row!). It is easy to see why. No one likes to be so easily dismissed. No one likes to be confronted with the fact that their words and opinions simply do not matter to the person to whom they are trying to express themselves. "Whatever" is an opportune (and simple) mantra from our culture that has become quite adept at dismissing anything and everything. "Whatever" is a great tool to avoid critical thinking and giving strong consideration to truth.

One of the most costly social developments of our culture is the "whatever" attitude to marriage, sex, and relationships. Our culture (and in large measure, the church) has become flippant to divorce, same-sex marriage, cohabitation, sexual promiscuity, adultery, pornography, and any other evil you can devise. The response from our culture is not a robust discussion of competing ideas but a "whatever" attitude. Everything is now okay.

This attitude must be contagious because it seems as if the church has caught it. While there is a day coming quickly when we believe the worldly will be awakened, shed their flippant attitude, and attack the percepts of God with more vigor than we have witnessed, the Church seems content to stand idly by. The spiritual condition of the world is easy to discern, but what about the people of God. Why have we been flippant with these issues?

Jesus confronts a flippant attitude about marriage found among the religious leaders in His day. We see that as we examine the passage from Mark 10. Jesus, as He often did, was teaching the crowd. We do not know if He was specifically speaking about marriage or if that was simply the topic that the Pharisees wanted to use to trip Him up. However, they came, we are told, specifically to test Him. The religious leaders, by this time in Jesus' ministry, were tired of His teachings and the fact that there were large crowds who had come to see Him wherever He went. They were seeking for some manner in which they might test Him or trip Him up. This would have allowed them to either prove His ministry fake or give them cause to arrest Him. Jesus is, however, unfazed by this question. He returns their inquiry with a question of Him own.

It is important to note that when they asked what was lawful, they were not considering simple civil law. The civil law was largely unimportant to this debate. In a time where the civil law was not definitively set by the religious authorities, it should be irrelevant to the opinion of the religious leaders what the civil law says. Jesus asked them to explain what Moses had said. Moses was the great law giver and it would have been important to know what Moses had instructed. The reply is clear: **"Moses allowed a man to write a certificate of divorce and to send her away."** That seems clear enough. Moses apparently said that the dissolution of a marriage was easy. Write your wife a note and send her away.

This is the thought on divorce in our culture. Visit a lawyer and take care of the problem. Quick and easy. Moses' words bring even more clarity to the opinion of the Pharisees in Deuteronomy 24:1. **"When a man takes a wife and marries her, if then she finds no favor in his eyes because he has found some indecency in her, and he writes her a certificate of divorce and puts it in her hand and sends her out of his house, and she departs out of his house.**

That seems to be fairly straightforward. If she finds no favor in your eyes you can send her on her way. No big fuss there. Our culture has adopted this mantra for divorce. "Do what feels right." "Make yourself happy." We understand that marriage is now of little value to our culture and the Pharisees seemed to be sharing in the devaluation of marriage. Marriage is seen as a personal choice and no longer a foundation of the community.

Followers of Christ are often told that the sexual revolution and our culture's attempt to redefine marriage has no effect on the marriage values of Christians. In this, those who espouse that idea are mistaken. Any attempt to devalue marriage, in any society, has consequences for the entire society. When a society changes the definition of marriage to include persons of the same gender and/or increase the number of persons included in the bond, they are telling their citizenry and the world that marriage has no firm definition. It is something that is so unimportant, it can be changed on a whim. George Barna, after a 2008 study on marriage, concluded:

> There no longer seems to be much of a stigma attached to divorce; it is now seen as an

unavoidable rite of passage. Interviews with young adults suggest that they want their initial marriage to last, but are not particularly optimistic about that possibility. There is also evidence that many young people are moving toward embracing the idea of serial marriage, in which a person gets married two or three times, seeking a different partner for each phase of their adult life.[1]

As believers, we must hold to a higher understanding of marriage than those Pharisees who felt enabled to dispose of a wife with a certificate and those in our society who believe marriage can be defined by whatever flavor five members of the Supreme Court determine is in vogue this week. We must value marriage and we do that, in part, by our understanding of divorce.

We must consider if we have become flippant in our understanding of marriage. Is it really so easy to end a marriage? Is it so easy to change the definition of marriage? The Pharisees wanted an easy out to marriage? Do you? Have you decided

---

[1] https://www.barna.org/barna-update/article/15-familykids/42-new-marriage-and-divorce-statistics-released#.VcOWnflViko

to forgo the commitment of marriage but partake in the sexual expressions that God has created to be enjoyed only between a husband and wife? As a believer in Christ, these are issues of great importance. We may have little control over our culture and may daily see the influence of the church waning. We do, however, have control over our obedience to the Word of God when it comes to our sexual and relational choices. Our Savior has spoken to us and all of His creation about sex, marriage, and divorce. We, as His children, would do well to listen. If we are disobedient and flippant in these areas, how will we impact our culture and point them toward their Creator?

3

HARD HEARTS

Henry VIII[2] was King of England from 1509-
1547. Henry VIII was a man with a hard heart.
Married six times, he was willing to take an entire
country of Catholics away from the Catholic
Church to end his first marriage and consummate
lustful desires. His second wife found herself
headless in the tower of London and a third never
lived to watch her son grow from a boy. His fourth
and fifth were short-lived and his sixth wife nursed
him until his death. History, as it often does, has
attempted to clean up his image, but in the end, he

---

[2] http://www.bbc.co.uk/history/people/henry_viii/

was a man with a hard heart.

When he married the wife of his late brother, she was unable to produce him a male heir. While this was obviously important for a king, it only served to harden his heart toward his wife. It also served to turn his desires toward another woman. Soon he was appealing to the Pope for an annulment so that he could take another wife. When the Pope refused, he married Anne Boleyn in secret, was excommunicated, and was subsequently setup as the Head of the Church of England. Within three years Anne Boleyn was publically executed because she had "lost favor" with Henry VIII.

Henry went on to marry Jane Seymour who gave him a male heir, though she died after childbirth, a high price to give the king his son. Henry then married a German princess, but they divorced after only a few months. Henry blamed his spiritual advisor for the breakup and executed him.

At almost fifty years old, he married a teenager but alleged she had previously had relationships with members of his court. She was executed. He finished out his life with his sixth wife who cared for him in his final days.

What a sad life he must have led. His hard heart at lead to the destruction of so many lives. He was so flippant about marriage and divorce that he was willing to break with his church to justify his lustful desires. He was willing to denounce the authority of the Pope not for theological reasons, but to justify his adulterous heart.

The Pharisees Jesus interacted with in Mark 10 were not afraid to reveal the hardness of their hearts. Their understanding of both divorce and Moses' words paint an incomplete picture. Their answer, and even Moses' proclamation, seem to stand in contrast to God's design for marriage. Is it really that simple? Is marriage simply a piece of paper? Can it really be ended by handing your spouse a subsequent piece of paper? Jesus' response stands in contrast to the Pharisees' understanding: **And Jesus said to them, "Because of your hardness of heart he wrote you this commandment.** Moses had given them this commandment because they were sinners and as sinners their hearts were hardened, even in their understanding of marriage. The law was given to reveal to God's people how truly wicked they were. Therefore, Moses gave them this ability to step away from their marriages because they had hard, sinful hearts and could not truly exemplify God's design for marriage.

In Jesus' day, it is clear that divorce was fairly easy. There were two differing opinions on what constituted the "some indecency" phrase of Deuteronomy 24:1. One was that it had to be moral lapse that would allow the husband to divorce his wife. The other opinion understood that anything that could be seen as offensive against the husband was justification to issue a "certificate of divorce." The main problem with both of these views is the underlying assumption that God, by putting in place provisions for divorce because of man's sinful nature, was condoning the practice. God was reacting to divorce in a similar manner to His reaction to the request of the Nation of Israel to have a king (1 Samuel 8). Why would they need a king when they had a King whose excellencies were far above any king that Samuel could ever find for them? In the same manner, why is it that men would need have provisions for a divorce? God was the very one who established marriage and had stated that it not be dissolved (Deuteronomy 24:9). However, since it was obvious that in man's fallen state divorces would occur, God made a provision for man's sinfulness. It is important to remember that God states clearly through the prophet Malachi that He hates divorce (Malachi 2:16) and that has not changed. He, just as He did with a king, allowed for divorces to be granted. It is clear, however, in both the Old and New Testaments, He does not condone them, puts strong stipulations on when they can be used, and does not mitigate the consequences of divorce.

Is your heart hard? Have your experiences made you callous toward divorce, marriage, and sexuality? Do you feel as though these are areas where no one has the authority to speak into your life? Do you see the Bible's teachings on these areas to be outdated and old fashioned? If this is the case, you would do well to examine again, carefully, what God has to say to these men who have such hard hearts. It is only because of the hardness of our hearts that there is any provision for divorce at all.

God's design was a creation void of any sexual sin. Creation showed a man and a woman, joined together by God, living in perfect union. The hardness caused by sin made it necessary for God to put provisions in place to continually reveal to us our devastated state apart from Him. If you find your heart hardened toward God's plan for sex and marriage and His abhorrence of divorce, cry out to Him. Seek His face in prayer. Pray for a clean heart—a heart of flesh attuned to His voice. Search His Word. Do not buy into the lie that God does not care about the design and actions of a marriage. Do not believe for a minute that He is unconcerned about your sexual identity, expressions, and actions. He created you! He knows you much better than you know yourself. He knows the hardness of your heart and His desire is the your heart of stone would become a heart born again in His image and reflecting His glory.

4

GOD'S DESIGN FOR MARRIAGE

We were reading an article[3] recently about a Dairy Queen® that is very different from the others you may have visited. If you do not know, Dairy Queen® is a chain of ice cream focused restaurants. Just writing that makes us want to go visit one. When we were kids, the only two Dairy Queen's® even remotely close were small buildings with no seating inside. To be served, you would walk up to the counter, order the ice cream, and either eat it standing in front of the restaurant or return to your car to consume the heavenly goodness. Now,

---

[3] http://www.nhregister.com/business/20150801/this-dairy-queen-has-an-original-flavor-that-customers-love

you can find many more Dairy Queens®, and most of them now have a place to sit down and also offer and expanded menu with hotdogs, hamburgers, and other items.

The article we read was about a particular Dairy Queen® in Moorhead, Minnesota that is bucking the system. Like most chain restaurants, you can go into almost any Dairy Queen® and find the same menu items, the same sizes, and the same flavors of ice cream. This particular Dairy Queen®, however, marches to the beat of its own drum. Because the restaurant is still operating under a contract from the 1940s, they are able to avoid complying with many of the directives that are handed down from cooperate Dairy Queen®. The articles reveals that:

> While newer contracts stipulate adherence to strict corporate guidelines, messaging and menus, the Moorhead shop still operates mostly under the terms of a contract signed in 1949. And that allows owners Troy and Diane DeLeon the freedom to dish out what might be considered rogue menu items.
> There's the Mr. Maltie, a chocolate malt on the stick; the Monkey Tail, a chocolate-covered

frozen banana; and of course the Chipper Sandwich, which is vanilla ice cream sandwiched between two chocolate chip cookies and dipped in chocolate.

The DeLeons also offer unique toppings, some of which have been discontinued by headquarters, as well as noncorporate approved food items, including barbecue sandwiches and Polish sausages. And the ice cream cakes? Let the other shops take HQ's premade cakes; Troy DeLeon assembles his himself.[4]

Now, while this sounds amazing to us and apparently to the 1,200 plus people who showed up in subzero temperatures to opening day of this Dairy Queen® location this past spring, the folks at cooperate do not think it is that great. Dean Peters, the spokesman for Dairy Queen® said, "the company cannot promote the store 'as a brand and a system,' and added that most DQ® lovers are looking for uniformity and the indoor dining experience provided by the company's newer DQ® Grill and Chill restaurants."[5]

---

[4] Ibid.

[5] Ibid.

The Beautiful Design

The cooperate bosses have a design for Dairy Queen®. They have based the decision on studies and research. Most of us, when we go into a chain restaurant, expect that they will have the same menu items no matter where we are. I (Micheal) have eaten a Dairy Queen® Blizzard® in a small town in a northern, remote region of a South Asian county and I can tell you it tasted just like one I would eat here in North Carolina. This small Dairy Queen® location, however, has apparently found a winning formula in their community. Who is right? Does it really matter?

When it comes to ice cream, the answer is largely unimportant. We have had ice cream from both a traditional Dairy Queen® and a new DQ® Grill and Chill. They are both, frankly, awesome. Both designs work and are successful.

Marriage, however, is not something where each person can do that which is right in his/her own eyes. God has a plan for marriage. He has a design that has been made clear. Jesus reminds them of this design when He says: **But from the beginning of creation, 'God made them male and female.' 'Therefore a man shall leave his father and mother and hold fast to his wife, and the two shall become one flesh.' So they**

are no longer two but one flesh. What therefore God has joined together, let not man separate." God's design for marriage is permanence. Not something that is short-term; not something that we seek to get out of. Jesus is quoting here from the book of Genesis. The commands for marriage are given before the Fall of Genesis 3. They are commands given to Adam and Eve, and reflect the beauty of the first marriage. Whereas the Fall and our sinful nature resulted in Moses' rules for divorce, God's generous gift to our first parents was a beautiful, perfectly designed marriage where they became one flesh. No longer two distinct people, but one.

The core of the Bible's teaching on marriage and divorce is about the oneness of marriage. If you think about root cause of divorce, it is the lack of this oneness that destroys marriages. Whether you have been divorced or have witnessed its destructive nature from the outside, divorce is caused by the absence of the two being one flesh. When a man and a woman do not see themselves as one, their relationship is doomed. Whether they start out their marriage thinking this way, or slip back into old thoughts of prioritizing himself or herself over their spouse, nothing good can come from a failure to be one. So what is oneness?

It would be easy to hear this passage and limit your thinking here to the sexual relationship between husband and wife. That would, however, be a shallow way to understand this text. It is true that most people have already involved themselves in sexual relations design exclusively for marriage long before ever making a commitment before God. The Scriptures are clear: sex is a good creation of God made exclusively for the marriage of a man and a woman. Anything apart from that is sin and a distortion of God's perfect design.

At the same time, the oneness that Genesis (which by the way, Moses wrote) and Jesus describe extends far beyond the marriage bed. When we consider divorce, it is always a breakdown of oneness. Whether there is adultery, violence, greed, pride, or some other issue that is attributed to the breakdown of a marriage, the absence of oneness lies at the heart of the issue. A wife does not cheat on her husband when they are one flesh. A man is not violent toward his wife when the two are one.

Our culture and our sin attempt to tell us that we can be married and yet distinct. That we can look out for our own interests above those of our spouse. Friends, this is not the case. Should you view your own interests as more important than those of your marriage, you will find yourself facing the end of that union. This is a sad and dangerous mistake to make. God calls us to complete unity with our spouse. We are to be one in our money, the care of our children, our priorities, our goals for the future. We need to be one in our worship, prayer, and our desire for the things of the Father.

Jesus tells the crowd that has gathered around Him: **What therefore God has joined together, let not man separate."** Marriage is not a manmade institution. Sinful men and women have taken God's perfect creation and destroyed it. We have made it a simple matter to separate what God has placed together. We should not be surprised by this. Most people who get married think nothing of God when they join together and therefore nothing about Him when they part ways. Craig Evans writes, "Divorce, then, no matter how nuanced its defense or how cleverly justified, violates God's design for human marriage."[6] When a man and a woman divorce, no matter the reason, something that God has put together has been broken. How ironic that a marriage inaugurated before a pastor and a church is terminated under the rule of judges and lawyers. This is far from the design of our Creator.

Do you understand God's design for marriage? More importantly, have you committed yourself to God's design for your marriage? This means committing to be one with your spouse no matter what arises. This means that you will refrain from any sexual activity outside of your marriage. This means if you are a woman you will commit yourself to your husband. You will be his and only his. You will never leave him or forsake him. You will care for him and put his needs above your own. If you are a man, the same applies. You will be hers and only hers. You will never leave her or forsake her. You will care for her and put her needs above your own. The two of you will seek to be one. You will set your separateness aside

---

[6] Craig Evans. *Mark 8:27-16:20*. World Biblical Commentary. 34B. 2001. 85.

and pick up the oneness that God designed and demands of a marriage.

This is God's good design for marriage. Anything less than one man and one woman is a distortion. Anything less is something other than marriage. As Christians, we should love God's design for marriage because it is good. It is not only good, but beneficial for us, our culture, and His Kingdom.

5

THE CONSEQUENCES
OF DIVORCE

The flow of the world is driven by choices and consequences. Our world is very orderly. We understand as Christians that there are times when God intervenes into human history and the unexplainable happens. However, for the most part, things follow a pattern and flow that God put in place at Creation.

Normally, as we grow older, we are better able to evaluate our choices and understand the consequences thereof. Often we will take more time to avoid risks and minimize unwanted consequences the older we get. What is often difficult, no matter our age or experience, is to weigh out unforeseen or belated consequences. We may be able to weigh the first or even fiftieth consequence of our actions but it is those that are immeasurable that will often cause us the most pain. It is the unexpected gust of wind that takes the field goal kicker's attempt wide right as time expires in the championship game. It is the poor soul who drops to one knee to propose to his girlfriend on the night she had planned to end their relationship. The butterfly who flaps his wings one too many times and a hurricane devastates the East Coast of the US.

Actions have consequences. Some we are able to calculate in our decision making process. Others catch us unaware. If we had been able to put them in the equation formulated in our mind, we may have chosen differently. We are, however, stuck with those consequences. We simply have to live with them.

Ending a marriage is clearly one of these situations. There are innumerable known consequences when a marriage ends. The one union becomes two broken hearts. Two homes. Two identities. Two lives no longer going in the same direction. Children no longer have parents who are one, but two people who have to simultaneously carry on two roles when their children are present and feel an emptiness when the children are elsewhere. These consequences can be seen long before a marriage is dissolved.

There are, however, those belated consequences. The ones you cannot calculate ahead of time. Did you know someone who is divorced is more likely to have serious debt that someone married?[7] Or consider this from Paul Amato, a researcher at Penn State University:

Research during the last decade continued to show that children with divorced parents, compared with children with continuously married parents, score lower on a variety of emotional, behavioral, social, health, and academic outcomes, on average. Similarly, adults with divorced parents tend to obtain less education, have lower levels of psychological well-being, report more problems in their own marriages, feel less close to their parents (especially fathers), and are at greater risk of

---

[7] https://www.barna.org/barna-update/culture/624-how-the-last-decade-changed-american-life#.VcOX3flViko

seeing their own marriages end in divorce.[8]

We have to imagine that these are not calculated but belated consequences of divorce. Sad realities in a culture that puts individual happiness above all else. Children are often forced to simply deal with whatever happens. They become the victims of the consequences.

However, children are not the only victims of divorce. Divorce has long lasting effects on both members of the former couple.[9] There are long lasting financial, emotional, sexual, and relational effects for all victims of divorce.

Jesus wanted his disciples to understand the effects and consequences of divorce. When He and His disciples had returned to the place they were staying, the disciples want further information. They are coming out of a culture

[8] Amato, P. R. (2010), Research on Divorce: Continuing Trends and New Developments. Journal of Marriage and Family, 72: 650–666. doi: 10.1111/j.1741-3737.2010.00723.x

[9] Amato, P. R. (2000), The Consequences of Divorce for Adults and Children. Journal of Marriage and Family, 62: 1269–1287. doi: 10.1111/j.1741-3737.2000.01269.x

where divorce was easy. They had witnessed their friend (and for some of them former mentor) John the Baptist killed for decrying that a divorce and remarriage involving King Herod was unlawful. Now Jesus had weighed in and He was as equally staunch in His stand for marriage as John had been. He reveals to them in verses ten through twelve the high standard for the people of God. This should not be surprise us. Jesus makes it clear throughout the Gospels His standards for the people of God. He tells His disciples that hatred in their heart was the same as murdering. If they had lust toward someone, they had committed adultery with that person.

With this in mind, it is not out of character for Jesus to make the strong statements in the final verses of our text. Jesus' answer stands in stark contrast to the sentiment of the Pharisees: **He answered, "Anyone who divorces his wife and marries another woman commits adultery against her. And if she divorces her husband and marries another man, she commits adultery."** In Jewish law, remarriage was only valid if the cause of divorce was valid. Jesus is making that clear here. If His disciples were to avoid initiating divorce, it is no surprise that Jesus declares that simply ending a first marriage on paper, does not alleviate the one-flesh, for-life design made by God. There is much debate about what situations the Bible grants as acceptable for divorce. We do not go into them here, because that is far from the purpose of this book or our passage from Mark's Gospel. God hates all divorce from the most serious cause to the most trivial. God hates all things that break his beautiful design! Regardless of the cause for a divorce, we understand that two lives that have been so intimately joined together are not easily separated.

Jesus tells us in this text that when one spouse abandons the other and then takes another spouse, he has violated God's law and committed adultery against the first spouse. This reminds us that you can never think that a judge and lawyers can end what has been joined together in God's eyes. Divorce is serious with deep consequences for all who are involved.

If you are considering divorce, have you weighed the consequences. Have you considered what will happen to your children? Have you pondered what is to become of their future relationships as a result of your decision? What about your spouse? Have you considered what you are about to do to them? Are you ready to destroy many lives on your path to happiness?

Before all of that, have you considered what God has said about your marriage? Do you know how important it is to Him? Do you know that His design is for happiness and contentment in your marriage? However, it must be done in the context of His design. Divorce has consequences that will abound for the remainder of your life. Our God is gracious to us when dealing with all of our sin, including divorce. We however, should not be unaware that His grace does not remove the consequences of every one of our decisions. Divorce has terrible consequences of which we should be keenly aware.

6

MOVING FORWARD

The church has a poor track record when it comes to marriage and divorce. Unfortunately, divorce has transitioned from taboo to normal. We believe this has led to the epidemic of cohabitation, the legalization of same-sex marriage, and a nation where the average young person has had sex by 17 years old but does not marry until their mid-twenties. The church will struggle to speak to these sexual sins when our closets are full of our unconfessed sexual sins. We have to be serious about marriage and divorce. We have to confess where we have sinned. We cannot write it off as acceptable and inevitable. We want you to consider some practical and philosophical applications for our churches and our marriages:

COMMIT TO MARRIAGE
Commit to yourself, your spouse, the church, and most importantly to Christ that divorce is not an option for you.

There are many in our society who begin to check out what might be available to them if they leave their spouse long before ever filing for a divorce. They want to know what options they have. They have struggles in their marriage and it causes them to begin to look to who else might be available. We have spoken with married people who claim the name of Christ and yet are looking to future marriages instead of giving attention to the problems they are dealing with in their current marriage. That is sin, conjured up in the pits of Hell to destroy your marriage and bring shame on the name of Christ. Divorce is very serious in our Lord's eyes. Consider these words from the prophet Malachi. God had judged His people harshly and the prophet tells them why: **And this second thing you do. You cover the Lord's** altar with tears, with weeping and groaning because he no longer regards the offering or accepts it with favor from your hand. But you say, "Why does he not?" Because the Lord was witness between you and the wife of your youth, to whom you have been faithless, though she is your companion and your wife by covenant. Did he not make them one, with a portion of the Spirit in their union? And what was the one God seeking? Godly offspring. So guard yourselves in your spirit, and let none of you be faithless to the wife of your youth. "For the man who does not love his wife but divorces her, says the Lord, the God of Israel, covers his garment with violence, says the Lord of hosts. So guard yourselves in your spirit, and do not be faithless" (Malachi 2:13-16).

God judges them because they have treated marriage with low regard. Commit yourself, regardless if you are unmarried, struggling in your marriage, or divorced to treat marriage in the highest regards! Commit, if you have never been married, that you will be a one-marriage person. If you are married, rule divorce out as an option.

If you are divorced but are planning to remarry, let your future spouse know that you have no plans to ever divorce them. That there will be no more marriages for you. If they cannot commit the same, flee!

GUARD YOUR HEART
Do not spend time alone with members of the opposite sex outside of your family.

Here is a good question to ask: "Would my spouse be okay with the time I am spending with this person and the topics of our conversations?" If you have any reservations about the answer to that question, you have your answer as to what you should do. We understand that in your work place it may be impossible to avoid this one hundred percent of the time. However, you know yourself and your heart. Your job is not worth destroying your marriage. If you cannot control yourself in your workplace, get another job! If you trust yourself completely with members of the opposite sex, you have already started down a dangerous road. Beware! When we become comfortable, we have already exposed ourselves to a dangerous and unnecessary temptation. No friendship, with anyone, no matter how important it may seem to you, is worth even straining your marriage. Guard your heart! Avoid the temptation. This goes for husbands and wives equally. You are not strong enough to resist the temptations that we all face each and every time. The more often you can avoid those temptations, the easier it will be for your to avoid Satan's trap. Do not ruin your life over the temporary satisfaction of sinful desires.

If you are unmarried, but in a relationship with someone of the opposite sex, you should limit the time you spend with them alone. God cares about your sexual purity before marriage just as much as He does once you are married. If you are in a relationship that does not respect that you want to save all sexual expressions for marriage, you are not with someone worthy to marry a son or daughter of King Jesus. Defend your honor and the honor of the Kingdom of Christ by reserving all sexual activity for your marriage.

BE VIGILANT

If you have already experienced divorce and remarriage, be vigilant!

Friends, Satan is crouching at your door. He loves to destroy marriages. He loves to break up families. And if you are on a second or third or fourth marriage, he is waiting to devour you like a lion. It does not matter if your previous marriage was before you were a Christian or if you or your spouse fell into sin, he is waiting. He wants to remind you of the failures of before. He wants to remind you of the time when your marriage did not make it. Combat his attack with vigilance! Be alert! Do not let him catch you being lax in your marriage. Put in the work that may have not been present the first time around. Commit yourself to your spouse and to constantly improving your marriage. Think back to the second marriage of Henry VIII mentioned in chapter three. He was quick to dismiss his first wife so that he could marry the object of his sexual desire. He led England out of the Catholic Church and set himself up as the head of the church so that he could divorce and marry a women he had already impregnated. For him, it seemed the best solution. The second time would be better. Anne Boleyn ended up beheaded and Henry married four more times. He demonstrated that it can get easier to stray into sin. Social scientists describe this as "serial marriage." It has become assumed that you can simply dispose of the one before and find someone "greater" and "better." This was Henry VIII's attitude and he left a wake of destruction in his path. Guard your heart against this attitude. Guard your heart against lustful temptations. Commit yourself to making sure the pain of divorce does not rear its ugly head in your life again.

CONSIDER YOUR CALLING
If you are divorced and not remarried, consider whether remarriage is something God has for your or if His desire is that you remain single.

This one may be the one that cuts the deepest. For the world, there is no question in this. Again, "do what feels right" is the mantra of the day. However, is that what God really desires. God takes marriage, divorce, and remarriage very seriously. If you are His child and you have experienced the pain and destructive nature of divorce, it is wise for you to give strong consideration to His Word before seeking to once again marry.

Can godly remarriages happen? We believe so. Should remarriage of divorced persons happen as frequently as it does? We think not. As calloused as many are to the danger and consequences of divorce, we think many are even more oblivious to the care that must be prevalent in remarriage. We are amazed at the celebrities that are remarried within months of divorce. They seem to have no thought of the factors that have just resulted in a terrible tragedy and they stand poised to assist history in repeating herself.

As believers in the Sovereign King who has made all things, including marriage, we should approach all remarriages with diligence and caution. We should examine what caused the first marriage to terminate. What caused you and your spouse to move away from each other? What caused the destruction of the oneness that God created when you were married? Did you ever really allow Him to create oneness?

We encourage you to spend a large amount of time in prayer. Seek counsel from a godly pastor and from other Christians who have marriages that display God's glory. Invite them to examine your previous marriage—to help you understand what happened and how God desires to work. Do not rush in or we fear that you may find yourself experiencing further heartache. Neglect here may result in continued destruction in your relationships.

HONOR MARRIAGE
Healthy, biblical marriages are a cornerstone of a healthy, biblical church.

Hebrews 13 gives a pattern for health in the church. Verse four states, **Marriage should be honored by all, and the marriage bed kept pure, for God will judge the adulterer and all the sexually immoral.** The church suffers when marriage suffers. The church is not able to carry out her mission when the families that comprise her are falling apart. We need healthy marriages to help sustain the healthy church. Healthy marriages often result in healthy families. This is good news for the continuation of the church.

Does your church value marriage? So many churches have ceased to hold marriage in high regard. They have adopted the view of marriage held by our culture. They no longer value the biblical concept of one man and one woman, married for life. They do this in contradiction to the precious Word of God and to the detriment of their effectiveness for the Kingdom of God. If you are in a church that has devalued marriage, get out! We would be willing to guarantee you they have devalued other aspects of God's Word.

The writer of Hebrews reminds us that marriage should be valued by all! If you are a leader in your local church, lead you church to value marriage. Help others in your church see the value of marriage. Encourage your pastor and other leaders to give attention to the marriage of your congregation. Encourage those who are struggling in their marriage. Adopt them. Pray for them. Serve them. Do this and see how God will honor your efforts.

We describe in chapter seven the picture that the Gospel paints of our marriages and how our marriages paint a picture of the Gospel for those around us. Our churches should work hard to disciple our people toward that end. Everyone in our church should know the Gospel image of their marriage.

SEEK GRACE
God's grace is greater than divorce.

We should not be flippant about divorce. Our world is has become numb to divorce. It is anticipated that every marriage will end in divorce—it is understood as normal. We understand that marriage is sacred. We hold marriage in high regard. We believe marriage is forever. However, we also understand that God's grace extends to those who have experienced divorce. Divorce is not the end of your usefulness for Christ's Kingdom. Divorce does not prevent you from Christ's salvation.

Those who have experienced divorce need God's grace. They are hurting. Often divorce can drive a wedge between them, their relationship with Christ, and their involvement in the life of the church. God's grace, however, abounds to all those who cry out to him in repentance and in faith.

If you have experienced divorce, lean on the grace of the great Savior of the universe. He stands ready to welcome you with open arms. He stands ready to fill the holes left because of the destruction of your relationship. Christ is the good God who took upon Himself all sins—including the sin of divorce—as He hung upon the cross, cursed with the wrath of a holy God. Because of this, we can experience His grace.

If you have been divorced, have you sought God's grace? Do not dismiss this important need. Do not go through life with your relationship with our heavenly Father strained because you have not pursed His grace. He stands ready to extend it, but we fear too many believe it is not necessary. Bask in His grace and see if it is not a beautiful place to reside.

7

THE GOSPEL IN MARRIAGE

Christ follower, do you know why marriage is so important? To hear the world's version of our beliefs, we are simply homophobic, old-fashioned, bigots. We are stuck in another century and a belief system that is outdated. However, this is a gross misunderstanding. We have a high view of traditional, one-man-and-one-woman-for-life-marriage because it is a picture of the beautiful mystery of Christ and His Church. Paul writes to the church at Ephesus about marriage: **This**

mystery is profound, and I am saying that it refers to Christ and the church (Ephesians 5:32).

The church is the bride that has been given to Christ, the perfect groom, by our Heavenly Father. Christ has been given His bride and no one can separate them. No one can snatch the bride from her groom. This picture shows us the wondrous nature of Christian marriage. Christ gave himself for His church. His bride had been captured by sin and separated from her first love. However, Christ laid down His life to purchase His bride.

The work of Christ must define our attitude toward and understanding of marriage. What God has joined together, we have no right to separate. We should treat our marriages as no more able to be separated than any one of us can be separated from Christ who has bought us with His blood.

We must understand our marriage in the context of the Gospel. Marriage was given in Genesis 2 to assist in our understanding of the Gospel today. This mystery that Paul describes is so invaluable for how we understand our marriage and in turn how we project our marriage to a watching world. Paul discusses marriage in his letter to the Ephesian church. The love and respect he prescribes for husbands and wives is intrinsically tied to the picture of Christ's sacrifice for the church. They cannot be separated. Marriage, therefore, is a picture of what God has done for us in Jesus Christ. Wives submit to their husbands as the church does to Christ and husbands give themselves up for their wives as Christ has done for His bride.

It is difficult to imagine the destruction of a marriage built with the Gospel in mind. While we am not naïve that there have been many marriages, built on this attitude, that have ended, we would suspect that many of them did so upon losing sight of the Gospel principles God has for marriage.

We should all strive for our marriages to reflect the Gospel. This is our only hope. Apart from the Gospel, there is no hope for sustained marriage. Without a proper understanding and practice of Gospel-focused marriage, we should suspect that our efforts to conjoin two lives that are different, selfish, and self-serving will fail. However, with Christ, there is hope.

When the Gospel is present, we are then afforded the opportunity to point others to the Gospel through our marriage. A Gospel-centered marriage is a radical notion. Oneness in Christ is a view out of the mainstream. When our marriages are a reflection of the Gospel and the power of what Christ has done for us on the cross, they will look very different from the relationships of the people around us. We will act differently toward our spouse than other people do. We will speak differently about our spouse when they are not around than other people do.

We all have the opportunity to take our marriages—reflections of the Gospel—and point those who see them back to the Good News of Christ. Your marriage is an opportunity for you to perpetuate the Great Commission. Your marriage can stand as a sign among your church, family, and community that the Gospel of Christ is true.

In our current culture, marriage is not esteemed. It is cheap and easy. It is not meant to last. It is only valuable if it makes us feel good. However, Christian marriage is designed to reveal to our culture that a holy God has created marriage. He has given it and all that it entails—companionship, children, sex, stability, and so much more—as a good gift to those who He created. While our world works every day to distort His perfect plan for marriage, we who are His children have been afforded the precious opportunity to purse Gospel-centered marriages, and in doing so point the world back to the one who has graciously given us this gift.

Would you pray with me for Gospel-centered marriages? Would you purse one with your spouse? Would you encourage them in your church? If you are unmarried, would you pray for your future spouse that he/she is committed to a Gospel-centered marriage, even now, even if you have not met? The only hope for this world is Christ. Praise God that He has called us to spread the Gospel of Christ, and thanks be to Him for calling us to do so through our marriages.

ABOUT THE AUTHORS

Micheal and Rachel have four sons, and three daughters. They make their home in Icard, NC where Micheal is the pastor of First Baptist Church. He has severed several other churches during thirteen years of vocational ministry.

He holds a B.A. in Theater Arts from Gardner-Webb University in Boiling Springs, NC, a Master of Christian Ministry from the T. Walter Brashier Graduate School at North Greenville University in Greer, SC. and a Doctor of Education from Southeastern Baptist Theological Seminary.

Micheal has had the privilege of speaking in churches, Baptist associations, colleges, and conferences across the U.S. and internationally.

He is the author of a number of books, including *It Shall Not Return Void*, *Pulling the Pieces Together*, *#OneAnother: Is the Social Media Phenomenom Shaping Our Relationships?*, and *Hear Now the Sower: The Rabbi and His Parable's Interpretation*.

Rachel holds a B.S. in Elementary Education from Gardner-Webb University in Boiling Springs, NC. She was a public school teacher for six years and now homeschools her children. She is active in the ministry at First Baptist Icard where she works with children's discipleship and Sunday school.

Made in the USA
Columbia, SC
23 October 2020